7 GOLDEN RULES FOR RETIREMENT PLANNING

7 Golden Rules For Retirement Planning

Emmanuel Zvada

Contents

Dedication

To those who are on the path to retirement, those who are embarking on this new journey, and those who have already embraced it.

This book is dedicated to you. Your experiences, wisdom, and stories have been my greatest inspiration. Your journeys and insights have illuminated the way for others, and I am deeply grateful for the lessons you have shared. Your future is my deepest inspiration, and I hope this book helps to ensure a secure and prosperous life for you. May you find guidance and wisdom in these pages as you navigate your own paths.

To my spouse, Lorraine thank you for your unwavering support and belief in me throughout this journey. Your encouragement has been a constant source of strength and motivation. Your love and understanding have been my anchor, and I am eternally grateful for your presence in my life.

To my Sisters, Aneni , Anashe and Colleta you are my greatest pride and joy. May this work reflect the values we hold and the legacy we strive to build together. May you find guidance and wisdom in these pages as you navigate your own paths.

To my parents, Esnath and Julius thank you for instilling in me the values of hard work, perseverance, and the importance of planning for the future. Your guidance has shaped who I am today, and I am forever grateful for your wisdom and love.

To my friends and colleagues, thank you for your support, feedback, and encouragement. Your insights and experiences have enriched this book and made it a more comprehensive resource for all who read it.

To The Methodist Church in Zimbabwe (MCZ) Connexional Office for arranging yearly training on Retirement Planning, City West Seventh Day Adventist and Borrowdale Church ,your insights during my presentation has contributed a lot to this book.

With heartfelt gratitude,

Acknowledgements

First and foremost, I would like to thank the Lord for His guidance and wisdom throughout the writing of this book. There is a verse in the Bible in Proverbs 13:22 (NKJV) which reminds us that, "A good man leaves an inheritance to his children's children, but the wealth of the sinner is stored up for the righteous." This verse has been a guiding light in my journey to understand and emphasize the importance of financial planning for retirement.

I am deeply grateful to my family for their unwavering support and encouragement. My spouse, Lorraine Nyasha Zvada has been my rock, offering invaluable insights and unwavering support during the writing process. My child, Talia, have been a source of inspiration, reminding me of the legacy we aim to leave behind.

I would also like to extend my heartfelt thanks to my friends and colleagues who have provided feedback, shared their experiences, and offered encouragement. Special thanks to Allen Gava for his invaluable contributions and for always being there when I needed a sounding board.

I am indebted to the many financial and retirement experts and authors whose work has informed and inspired this book. Their dedication to educating others about financial planning has been a beacon of knowledge and guidance.

Lastly, I am grateful to my readers. Your interest in this topic and your commitment to planning for a secure future are what drive me to share this knowledge. May this book serve as a helpful resource in your journey towards a fulfilling and financially secure retirement. Thank you all for your support and encouragement.

How to Use This Book

Welcome to "7 Golden Steps of Retirement Planning"! This book is designed to guide you through the essential steps to ensure a secure and prosperous retirement. To make the most of this resource, start by familiarizing yourself with the structure of the book, which is divided into seven key sections.

Utilize the provided worksheets and checklists to organize your thoughts and track your progress. These tools will help you assess your current financial situation, set specific retirement goals, create a detailed savings plan, track your investments and expenses, and plan for healthcare costs.

Remember, retirement planning is an ongoing process. Regularly review and update your plan as your circumstances change. The final chapter provides guidance on how to review and adjust your plan to ensure it remains relevant and effective.

While this book offers a comprehensive guide, consulting with a financial advisor or retirement planning professional can provide personalized advice and help you navigate complex financial decisions.

By following these steps and utilizing the resources provided, you can create a robust retirement plan that ensures a secure and fulfilling future. Happy planning!

About the Author

Emmanuel Zvada is a distinguished Managing Consultant and the Founder of Third Eye Africa Consulting Group, a leading consultancy firm specializing in Human Resources Management and Retirement Planning. With over two decades of experience in the field, Emmanuel has established himself as a thought leader and innovator, known for his ability to help organizations overcome performance challenges and achieve strategic goals.

In addition to his role at Third Eye Africa Consulting Group, Emmanuel is a co-founder of the Zimbabwe Institute of Retirement Planning, an institution dedicated to educating and empowering individuals to make informed decisions about their financial future. His passion for retirement planning stems from a deep commitment to helping people achieve financial security and a fulfilling retirement.

Emmanuel's expertise extends beyond the boardroom; he is a sought-after speaker, trainer, and author, known for his ability to distill complex concepts into actionable insights. His work has been featured in various industry publications, and he regularly contributes to discussions on Human Resources Management and Retirement Planning through seminars, workshops, and media appearances.

Through his consultancy and educational initiatives, Emmanuel continues to empower organizations and individuals alike, providing them with the knowledge and tools necessary to navigate the complexities of retirement planning successfully. His dedication to excellence and his unwavering commitment to helping others achieve their full potential have earned him a respected position in the industry.

Emmanuel is a certified World Human Resources Development Practitioner and is a Certified Retirement Planning Specialist. He is also an active member of several professional organizations, where he continues to advocate for best practices and innovation in Human Resources and retirement planning.

1

Why to Retire Early?

"And in the end it's not the years in your life that count. It's the life in your years."
- Abraham Lincoln

D id you know that over 60% of people over the age of 50 fear the loss of independence more than death itself? This startling statistic throws a stark light on a truth many of us shy away from confronting. Why does this fear loom so large in the hearts of so many?

Let's embark on a journey through the pages of '7 Golden Rules for Retirement Planning: The Blueprint for Happy, Healthy and Wealthy Living,' As a writer I saw many people struggle to plan their retirement all over the world. This book helps to dismantle the shackles of fear and replace them with a plan, blueprint for a future that brims with freedom and health, and wealth irrespective of age.

Retirement, traditionally seen as the sunset years of one's career, is increasingly becoming a sunrise moment for many. The concept of retiring early, once a far-fetched idea, is now a tangible goal for a growing number of individuals across the globe. But why the sudden shift? What makes early retirement so appealing? This chapter delves into the multifaceted reasons behind the allure of early retirement, exploring the financial, personal, and societal benefits it offers.

Imagine a life where your golden years shimmer with the promise of adventure, learning, and fulfillment, unburdened by the conventional dread of aging. A life where every sunrise brings not a day older but a day bolder. But how, you may wonder, can such a life be achieved? Armed with strategies that marry financial wisdom with the art of living fully, we'll chart a course through the realms of investment, health, and personal fulfillment. Imagine mastering the art of making your money work for you, so effectively that it fuels your passions and dreams. Picture a life where you wake up every day to new adventures, learning, and the sheer joy of being alive, without the shadow of financial worry.

*"Success is not the key to happiness. Happiness is the key to success. If you love what you are doing, you will be successful." - **Albert Schweitzer***

What if I told you that this life exists? You just need to uncover these secrets that thousands of millionaires have used all over the world. As if the secret blueprint is not secret at all but can be created with discipline and all the millionaires follow it at the same. Early retirement is not merely a final destination; it's a transformative journey marked by financial independence and personal development. The objective is not solely to retire early but to embrace a life rich in purpose, passion, and financial liberty.

Are you ready to step into a world where your golden years gleam with promise, adventure, and the freedom to live on your terms? Let's begin the new chapter of your life now as we explore a plethora of the strategies and steps required to achieve this goal in the chapters that follow. It is clear that early retirement is not just about the destination; it's about the journey of growth, discovery, and the pursuit of a life well-lived.

2

The Mindset for a Youthful Retirement

****

"Often when you think you're at the end of something, you're at the beginning of something else."
- Fred Rogers

A s the sun dips below the horizon, casting a golden hue over the landscape, one can't help but reflect on the passage of time. It's an inevitable journey, one that each of us is on, moving towards what many refer to as the golden years. As this chapter in life (aging) approaches, a significant issue arises and overshadows this vibrant phase of life. The problem? A mindset entrenched in ageism and stereotypes, which, if left unaddressed, risks turning these years into a period of decline rather than one of growth and fulfillment.

The primary challenge lies in the societal narrative that paints retirement and aging as a time of slowing down, of becoming less relevant. This narrative is not just damaging; it's also profoundly inaccurate. The consequences of adopting such a mindset are far-reaching. Individuals may find themselves succumbing to a self-fulfilling prophecy, where expectations of decline lead to decreased activity, social isolation, and even health issues. The vibrancy of life begins to fade, not because of age itself, but because of a mindset that doesn't challenge the status quo.

But what if there's a different path? A road less traveled that leads to a retirement filled with energy, purpose, and a zest for life? The solution lies in building a mindset of continuous growth, curiosity, and positivity. This mindset doesn't just happen; it's crafted through intentional actions and choices.

Evidence of the efficacy of this approach is found not just in research but in the stories of those who've embraced it. Take, for instance, the tale of Colonel Harland Sanders, who started franchising his chicken recipe at the age of 65 and didn't achieve significant success until his late 60s. Today, KFC is a global fast-food giant. Their experiences underscore a profound truth: a youthful retirement is not about denying aging but about embracing it with a spirit of adventure and openness.

While this strategy offers a blueprint, it's by no means the only path to a fulfilling retirement. Some may find solace in solitude, exploring the inner landscapes of meditation or writing. Others might discover a calling in mentorship, sharing their wisdom with younger generations. The key is to recognize that retirement is not a one-size-fits-all experience but a deeply personal journey that offers endless possibilities for those willing to explore them and that is where you begin your new adventure.

In the end, the mindset for a youthful retirement isn't about turning back the clock but about moving forward with an open heart and an eager mind. It's about recognizing that every sunrise offers a new opportunity for growth, connection, and joy. So, as you stand at the threshold of your golden years, ask yourself: What adventures await? How will you embrace this chapter of life with the curiosity of a child and the wisdom of the years?

This path is yours to choose. And remember, it's never too late to start living young and free.

In the next chapter, we will discuss the types of opportunities you can create after retirement.

3

Opportunities Awaiting in Retirement

"There is a whole new kind of life ahead, full of experiences just waiting to happen. Some call it 'retirement.' I call it bliss."
- Betty Sullivan

Retirement often marks the beginning of a new chapter in life, filled with opportunities that were perhaps sidelined during the busy years of career and family. This phase offers a unique blend of freedom, experience, and perspective that can be leveraged in numerous ways. Retirement creates promises of renewal, growth, and boundless opportunities. But what exactly are these opportunities that come with the, even as the calendar pages turn? Let's embark on a journey to uncover them one by one in this chapter.

A beginning of exploration, of rediscovering oneself, and of seizing the day in ways previously unimaginable is possible once you are free from any entitlement. Following is the list:

1. Pursuing, Hobbies or Projects
2. Volunteering and Community Service
3. Mentorship and Sharing Knowledge
4. Travel and Exploration

5. Health and Wellness
6. Starting a Business

Each of these points opens doors to fulfillment, happiness, and a profound sense of purpose. Let's explore them in detail.

Take, for instance, the story of Esnath, who at 50, began her journey with pottery, creating pieces that not only brought her joy but also became cherished gifts among her friends and family.

The gift of time that retirement brings can be shared generously with those in need. Volunteering offers a unique blend of giving and receiving; while you contribute to a cause greater than yourself, you also gain immeasurable satisfaction. Studies have shown that individuals who volunteer report higher levels of happiness and well-being.

Imagine dedicating a few hours a week at a local food bank or teaching literacy skills to adults. These acts of service enrich the lives of others and your own, knitting the fabric of community tighter.

With a treasure trove of life and professional experiences, retirees are perfectly positioned to guide the younger generation. Whether it's through formal mentorship programs or casual conversations, the wisdom imparted can pave the way for others' success.

Consider the story of Mr. Jacob, a retired engineer who volunteered at a local high school, helping students with their physics projects. His guidance not only helped students excel academically but also inspired them to pursue careers in engineering.

The world is a book, and those who do not travel read only one page. Retirement opens the chapter to exploration, to immersing oneself in new cultures, cuisines, and landscapes. Travel need not be extravagant; even local excursions offer fresh perspectives and invigorate the spirit.

Fadzayi and Allen, a couple, made it their mission to visit every national park in their country, capturing memories and a sense of adventure that became the highlight of their retirement years.

A life well-lived is a life lived in health. Retirement provides the time to focus on physical well-being through exercise, nutrition, and mindfulness practices. Joining a gym or yoga class, adopting a plant-based diet, or meditating daily can have profound effects on your health, extending the quality and quantity of your life.

James, who took up cycling at 55, found not just improved cardio-vascular health but also a passion that led him to cycle across several states, meeting new friends and challenging himself in ways he never thought possible.

As we traverse through these opportunities, retirement promises us the life of possibilities. It's a time to live with purpose, to connect deeply with others, and to explore the vast experiences of life.

Retirement is a vibrant beginning. A beginning that asks, "What will you discover today?" The answer lies within, waiting to be un-covered in the golden years of living young and living free.

In all the previous chapters, I have given a glimpse of retirement benefits. Now let's learn seven golden rules of retirement planning in the next few chapters.

4

Rule 1: Budgeting for the Golden Years

"A budget tells us what we can't afford, but it doesn't keep us from buying it."

- Willian Feather

T he golden years, a period rich with the promise of leisure and liberty, also bear the weight of financial foresight. How does one navigate this transition, ensuring a flow of comfort and care that lasts? The answer lies in crafting a budget that's as realistic as it is resilient, accounting for healthcare, leisure, and the unforeseen. This chapter is your compass.

Imagine a vessel, steadfast and secure, navigating the unpredictable seas of post-retirement life. Your goal is to captain this vessel, armed with a budget that ensures you not only survive but thrive. This budget is your map, charting a course through expenses expected and unexpected, ensuring your golden years gleam with the luster of freedom and fulfillment.

Before setting sail, one must ensure their ship is equipped. Gather your financial statements, an understanding of your expected income (including pensions, investments, and savings), and a list of anticipated expenses. Arm yourself with a budgeting tool that resonates with your level of comfort and expertise. Knowledge of your health-care options and costs is crucial, as is an awareness of your lifestyle desires and the expenses they entail.

First, assess your current financial landscape. Next, forecast your retirement expenses, integrating both fixed and variable costs. Following this, you'll align your income and savings with these expenses. The final frontier involves ongoing review and adjustment, ensuring your budget remains as dynamic as the life it supports. The following framework may help you to assess your budget.

1.: Start by pouring over your financial statements. What is your current income? What savings and investments lie at your disposal? Understanding where you stand today provides a solid foundation for tomorrow.

2.: Here, precision is key. List all anticipated expenses, categorizing them as either fixed (housing, insurance, utilities) or variable (travel, hobbies, gifts). Don't forget to include healthcare costs, which often increase with age. Consider using historical spending to inform your estimates, adjusting for expected changes in lifestyle.

3.: With your expenses laid bare, it's time to ensure your income and savings can cover them. This may involve reallocating investments or adjusting your spending habits. The aim is to find balance, ensuring your income streams flow robustly against the tide of expenses.

4.: The only constant in life is change. Regularly reviewing your budget, at least annually, allows you to adjust to life's unpredictabilities. This iterative process ensures your budget evolves alongside you, maintaining its relevance and resilience.

Embrace flexibility. Your needs and desires will shift, and so should your budget. Be wary of underestimating healthcare costs; they often prove to be the most unpredictable element of retirement spending.

How do you know if your budget holds water? The proof is in the living. Begin by following your budget closely for the first few months of retirement. Are you consistently overspending in certain categories? Do you find unexpected expenses cropping up? Adjust your budget accordingly, keeping in mind the goal of sustainable, comfortable living.

If you find your expenses consistently outpacing your income, it's time for a closer inspection. Consider consulting with a financial advisor to identify potential adjustments in your spending or savings strategy. Remember, the goal is not merely to survive your golden years but to thrive within them.

A budget for the golden years is more than a ledger of income and expenses; it's a living document that breathes life into your retirement dreams. With careful planning and ongoing adjustment, you can ensure that your retirement is marked not by financial worry, but by the freedom and fulfillment of a life well-lived.

Remember, the journey of a thousand miles begins with a single step. Let this blueprint guide you, step by step, toward the horizon of your dreams.

Now, let's move to the chapter on 'investment strategies for a lasting legacy' that will help you to sustain your retirement dream.

5

Rule 2: Investment Strategies for a Lasting Legacy

****

"Investing is a journey of self-discovery. It reveals your relationship with money, your tolerance for risk, and your ability to stay disciplined in the face of uncertainty."

- Jeremiah Say

This chapter solves this question: How do we sculpt a financial legacy that stands the test of time, ensuring our golden years and beyond are not just survived but thrived upon?

Creating a lasting legacy through strategic investments in retirement involves a thoughtful approach that balances growth, preservation, and philanthropy. The goal is to ensure that your wealth not only supports you during your retirement years but also leaves a lasting impact on causes you care about or future generations. Here are several investment strategies to consider for building a lasting legacy:

There are myriads of options when you venture into the realm of investments for retirement planning and that ranges from bonds to the vibrant alleys of stocks, not to mention the enigmatic realms of real estate and beyond. Herein lies our proposition: Diversified investment strategies, underpinned by a keen understanding of risk and growth, are the cornerstone of a lasting legacy.

The cornerstone of our exploration is the compelling tale of the stock market. The companies that vying for growth and innovation, offer the investor a chance to partake in the economic successes of these entities. Yet, as we delve deeper, the stock market's vibrancy is matched by its volatility.

Economic downturns, like the severe financial crisis of 2008, underscore the volatility inherent in financial markets. These challenging periods emphasize the importance of diversification as a strategy to safeguard investments. By spreading assets across different classes, such as bonds, which often behave differently than stocks, and real estate, which can provide both rental income and the potential for value appreciation, investors can reduce risk while maintaining opportunities for growth.

However, skeptics of diversification point to historical instances where it has not fully protected against losses. They cite examples, including the early 2000s, when both stocks and bonds experienced declines, suggesting that diversification might not always shield investors from market downturns.

We must not put all eggs in one basket hence diversification across asset classes must be a priority. This includes a mix of local and international investments, such as stocks, bonds, real estate, and possibly alternative investments like commodities or private equity. International diversification can help protect against local market volatility.

Investing in real estate can also provide a reliable source of income through rentals and may also yield significant returns through property value appreciation. Targeting properties located in expanding urban centers or popular tourist destinations can enhance the investment's potential. Nonetheless, it is crucial to perform extensive research and due diligence, considering the historical complexities surrounding property rights in the country.

Another avenue to create a legacy while benefiting from it is venturing into the agricultural sector. This sector not only offers a natural hedge against inflation but also presents opportunities for substantial returns on investment. Engaging in agriculture can take various forms, from direct investment in farming operations, where one can participate in the cultivation and sale of crops or livestock, to investing in agribusinesses, which support the agricultural sector through services, equipment, and processing. Such investments not only contribute to the investor's financial security in retirement but also play a vital role in supporting the local economy and ensuring food security.

Investing in the education of future generations is a profound way to create a lasting legacy. In the context of retirement planning, consider establishing education funds or trusts that can provide financial support for the educational needs of family members or community members. These funds can cover a wide range of educational expenses, from primary and secondary school fees to university tuition and vocational training programs. By investing in education, retirees can ensure that their legacy continues to impact generations to come, fostering a culture of learning, innovation, and opportunity.

To create investment strategies for a lasting legacy, currency diversification emerges as a prudent approach to safeguard against the risks associated with local currency devaluation. This strategy involves holding assets in various currencies, particularly those known for their stability in the global market. By diversifying currency holdings, investors can mitigate the potential losses that might arise from the depreciation of their domestic currency. It's advisable to explore investment opportunities denominated in stable foreign currencies, such as the US dollar, Euro, or Swiss Franc, as these can serve as a hedge and preserve the value of one's investments over the long term.

Concluding, the journey through the investment landscape reveals a truth as enduring as time itself: The construction of a lasting legacy is an art and a science. It demands a palette of diversified investments, a deep understanding of risk and reward, and an unwavering commitment to long-term growth. As we stand upon the threshold of our golden years, let us choose to embark on this journey with wisdom, courage, and the foresight to build a legacy that endures. For in the end, it's not just about the wealth we accumulate, but the future we sculpt for ourselves and the generations that follow.

In the next chapter, let's navigate on social security and pensions that assure you continuous income and cover your expenses.

6

Rule 3: Know Global Social Security and Pension

****

"Retirement isn't the end of the road, but just a turn in the road."
- Unknown

In the grand tapestry of retirement planning, the threads of social security and pensions weave through the fabric of global economies, offering a safety net to millions. Yet, the relevance and intricacies of these systems vary significantly from one country to another, reflecting the diverse socio-economic landscapes and governmental approaches worldwide. This chapter delves into the global relevance of social security and pensions, exploring their roles, challenges, and the navigation strategies for individuals in an increasingly interconnected world.

Social Security and pensions, those twin pillars of retirement income that promise a steady stream of support through the sunset years. At its core, Social Security is a governmental program designed to provide financial assistance to people in their retirement years, ensuring a measure of economic security and dignity. It operates on a simple principle: during your working years, you contribute a portion of your earnings into the system, and upon reaching a certain age, you begin to receive benefits based on your lifetime earnings.

Around the globe, social security and pension systems serve as cornerstones of retirement planning, aiming to ensure that individuals can maintain a decent standard of living post-retirement. These systems are financed and administered in various ways, ranging from government-sponsored and mandated programs to employer-based and private schemes. The level of benefits, eligibility criteria, and sustainability of these systems are influenced by a country's economic stability, demographic trends, and political will.

Social security and pension systems play a critical role in providing financial stability to retirees. Social security and pension systems serve as a crucial safeguard against the threats of poverty, disability, and unemployment, enabling individuals to cover their fundamental needs and experience their retirement years with dignity. However, the effectiveness of these systems in achieving this goal can vary significantly depending on the country's economic conditions and the design of its social security framework.

Once a cornerstone of retirement planning, traditional pensions have become rarer, relics of a bygone era. Pensions, or defined benefit plans, promise a specific monthly benefit at retirement, the amount of which is based on salary, years of service, and other factors. Unlike Social Security, the onus of contributing to the pension lies with the employer, not the employee.

For those fortunate to have a pension, understanding its terms is crucial. Does it adjust for inflation, ensuring your purchasing power remains constant through the years? What benefits does it provide to survivors? These questions paint the landscape of your financial future.

Despite their critical role in providing financial stability to retirees, social security and pension systems worldwide encounter numerous challenges. Among the most urgent are ensuring the long-term viability of funds amidst the global trend of aging populations, offering benefits that are sufficient to keep pace with escalating living expenses, and facilitating the seamless transfer of benefits for workers who have been employed in various countries throughout their careers. Furthermore, the intricate nature of navigating diverse social security systems can pose significant challenges for individuals with international work histories.

Consider John, a retired teacher with a pension. He must decide whether to opt for a higher monthly benefit that ceases upon his death or a slightly reduced benefit that continues to support his spouse. Each choice sketches a different future, illustrating the profound impact of seemingly minute decisions.

Social Security and pensions require a strategic approach. For many, consulting with a financial advisor can illuminate the path, turning the complex web of rules and regulations into a clear strategy for maximizing benefits.

Moreover, integrating these income streams into a broader financial plan is essential. For instance, if you delay Social Security benefits, how will you cover your expenses in the meantime? Perhaps you have savings, or maybe a part-time job fills the gap. Each piece of the puzzle must fit seamlessly together, crafting a picture of financial stability.

As we gaze into the horizon, the sustainability of Social Security and the rarity of pensions raise questions. Legislative changes may alter this picture significantly, affecting future retirees. Staying informed and adaptable is more than wise; it's essential. In an interconnected world, the relevance of social security and pensions transcends national borders, affecting the lives of millions. Understanding the global landscape, acknowledging the challenges, and adopting strategic approaches to navigate these systems are essential for securing a stable and comfortable retirement. As we look to the future, the evolution of social security and pensions will continue to shape the retirement landscape, offering both opportunities and challenges for individuals and policymakers alike.

The key takeaways are clear: understand your benefits, make strategic decisions, and integrate them into a comprehensive financial plan. As the final chapter of your working life closes, let the story of your retirement be one of security, comfort, and freedom.

Now, let's discuss pillars of physical health in the next chapter. As we know that good health helps us to enjoy our life to the fullest and this aspect becomes important in our retirement years.

7

Rule 4: The Pillars of Physical Health

****
"Take care of your body. It's the only place you have to live."
- Jim Rohn

As we age, maintaining vitality becomes more than a mere desire—it transforms into a vital necessity. The blueprint to a life lived both healthy, happy, and wealthy life during these years isn't shrouded in mystery but is instead built upon the foundational pillars of physical health: regular exercise, a balanced diet, and preventive healthcare. Each of these components plays a crucial role, acting as the bedrock for not only surviving but thriving in later life.

1. Regular Exercise
2. A Balanced Diet
3. Preventive Healthcare

Physical vitality begins with the commitment to regular exercise. But why is this so pivotal? The human body, a remarkable machine, thrives on movement. Exercise strengthens muscles, boosts heart health, and improves balance. It acts like key ingredients in achieving our health goal.

Studies have shown that seniors who engage in regular physical activity experience a lower risk of chronic diseases, improved mental health, and better cognitive function. The National Institute on Aging heralds exercise as a fountain of youth, capable of delaying the onset of many diseases associated with aging.

But how does one integrate exercise into daily life, especially when the golden years bring their share of physical limitations? The answer lies in finding joy in movement—be it through walking, swimming, yoga, or even gardening. Each step taken, each stroke swum, adds up, building a stronger, more resilient body.

Next, the importance of a balanced diet comes into view. Imagine the human body as a sophisticated engine; without the right fuel, its performance dwindles. A diet rich in fruits, vegetables, lean proteins, and whole grains acts as premium fuel, and that empowers the body to function at its best.

The science behind a balanced diet is compelling. According to the World Health Organization, proper nutrition reduces the risk of chronic diseases such as diabetes, heart disease, and cancer. But beyond statistics and studies, there's a simpler truth: eating well makes you feel good.

Incorporating a rainbow of foods into meals isn't just about health; it's also a celebration of flavors, textures, and memories. Food has the power to connect us to our past, to moments of joy, and to the possibilities of a vibrant future.

The final pillar, preventive healthcare, is the cornerstone of longevity. Regular check-ups, screenings, and vaccinations form a protective barrier against potential health issues, catching them before they blossom into major concerns.

The power of prevention is undeniable. For instance, the flu vaccine has been shown to significantly reduce hospitalizations among older adults. Moreover, screenings for conditions like breast and colorectal cancer can save lives through early detection.

But preventive healthcare isn't just about avoiding illness; it's about fostering a partnership with your healthcare provider. It's a commitment to listening to your body and taking proactive steps towards wellness.

In transitioning from one pillar to the next, a pattern emerges. Each is interconnected, supporting and enhancing the others. Together, they form a trinity of health that can guide us through the golden years with grace, strength, and vitality.

So, what does it mean to have a happy and healthy life in the context of our golden years? It means embracing these pillars of physical health with open arms and an open heart. It's about making conscious choices every day that honor our bodies and our journey.

But beyond the science, beyond the recommendations, there lies a deeper truth. The retirement years are not just a time to be endured but a stage of life to be savored, enriched by experiences, relationships, and the joy of living healthily.

As we close this chapter, a question lingers: How will you build your pillars of physical health? The blueprint is in your hands, the tools ready. It's time to construct a life that brims with vitality.

8

Rule 5: Mental Wellbeing and Emotional Balance

****

"Your emotions are the slaves to your thoughts, and you are the slave to your emotions."

- Elizabeth Gilbert

As we age, it becomes crucial for us to balance between mental and emotional well-being. While the previous chapters laid the foundation with physical health, it's essential to recognize that a truly vivacious existence in our later years also demands nourishment of the mind and soul.

Mental well-being demands us to stay socially connected, engage in mentally stimulating activities, and mindfulness practices that are not merely suggestions but the cornerstone of thriving as we age.

The assertion here is clear: nurturing mental health is paramount for a fulfilling life post-retirement. The evidence supporting this claim is both abundant and compelling. Research consistently shows that individuals who maintain strong social connections and engage their minds actively experience lower rates of cognitive decline and a higher quality of life. Furthermore, mindfulness practices have been linked to reductions in stress, anxiety, and symptoms of depression, enhancing overall emotional balance.

Diving deeper, let's consider the impact of social interaction. A study published in the American Journal of Epidemiology found that individuals with robust social ties had a significantly lower risk of mortality compared to those with weak or insufficient social relationships. This evidence underscores the life-extending power of connection, suggesting that our social lives are just as critical to our well-being as diet and exercise.

However, the path isn't without its obstacles. It's important to acknowledge that, for some, building and maintaining these connections in later life can be challenging. Age brings with it changes that can complicate social engagement, such as health issues, the loss of friends and loved ones, or even relocation.

Yet, this counterargument only highlights the importance of being proactive in fostering social ties, whether through community groups, volunteer work, or online platforms that can bridge the physical gap. The key is to remain open to new relationships and experiences, understanding that emotional flexibility can significantly enhance one's quality of life.

In addition to social connectedness, stimulating the mind through hobbies, learning, and creative pursuits offers another layer of protection against the mental decline often feared in older age. The adage "use it or lose it" finds real application here. Engaging in activities that challenge the brain, such as learning a new language, playing a musical instrument, or even puzzles, can create new neural pathways, keeping the mind sharp and agile.

Mindfulness and meditation offer a powerful counterbalance to the stresses and anxieties that can accompany aging. These practices anchor us in the present moment, promoting an awareness and acceptance that can lead to profound emotional healing and stability. The beauty of mindfulness is in its simplicity and accessibility; it requires no special equipment or environment, only the willingness to turn inward and observe the mind's landscape with compassion and non-judgment.

Envision a life where each day is greeted with a sense of purpose, curiosity, and connection. This vision is not only possible; it's within reach through the deliberate cultivation of mental well-being and emotional balance.

In conclusion, the blueprint for golden years filled with vitality and zest extends far beyond the physical. It demands attention to the mind and heart, fostering connections, engaging in mental gymnastics, and embracing the present with mindfulness. As we weave these practices into the fabric of our daily lives, we fortify ourselves against the challenges of aging, ensuring that our golden years are not only longer but richer and more rewarding. Let this chapter serve as a guide and an invitation to live a great life, with a mind and spirit as vibrant and resilient as the body we've learned to nurture and respect.

In the next chapter, we will explore how to pursue your passion and purpose after retirement.

9

Rule 6: Pursuing Passion and Purpose

****

"Finding what you're passionate about and using it to make a positive impact is the key to a fulfilling life".
- Ralph Kadurira

R etirement often conjures images of leisure and relaxation, a well-earned respite from the demands of work and career. However, for many, this phase of life also presents a unique opportunity to pursue long-held passions and purposes that may have been sidelined by professional responsibilities and the busyness of life. This chapter explores the concept of pursuing passion and purpose in retirement, offering insights, strategies, and inspiring stories of individuals who have transformed their retirement years into a vibrant journey of personal fulfillment and contribution.

As you retire, the days of your life are filled with different colors. What colors will you choose? What patterns will emerge out of it? The answer lies in the passions that ignite your spirit, the interests that have perhaps lain dormant, waiting for their moment in the sun. Identifying these passions is not just an exercise; it's the first step toward a vibrant, fulfilling retirement.

The first step in pursuing passion and purpose in retirement is self-discovery. This involves reflecting on your interests, values, and what brings you joy and fulfillment. It's about identifying those activities that you would do even if you didn't get paid for them. Once you've identified your passions, the next step is to consider how you can channel them towards a greater purpose, something that benefits others and contributes to the community or society at large.

Imagine waking each morning with a sense of purpose, eager to delve into activities that not only bring you joy but also challenge and fulfill you. This isn't a distant dream; it's a tangible goal. By the end of this journey, you'll have a clearer understanding of your interests and how to integrate them into your daily life. Let's follow the below point and explore it further.

- A quiet space
- A journal or notepad
- An open mind
- Willingness to explore

This journey unfolds in stages: reflection, exploration, deep dive, and integration. Initially, you'll look inward, reflecting on past joys and interests. Next, you'll explore these areas further, perhaps discovering new passions along the way. A deeper dive into these interests helps to understand their role in your life. Finally, you'll integrate these passions into your everyday existence, weaving them into your life.

1. Begin with introspection. Think back to your childhood, your young adult years, and your professional life. What activities made time stand still? Write these down, no matter how insignificant they might seem.

2. With your list in hand, select a few interests that spark curiosity. Do they still resonate? Explore them in whatever form possible—books, documentaries, courses, etc. Immersion brings clarity.

3. Choose one or two passions that stand out. Invest time in learning more. This could mean taking classes, joining clubs, or finding a mentor. The depth of your exploration will solidify your interest or perhaps redirect it.

4. Finally, integrate these passions into your daily schedule. Make your interests a priority.

- Stay flexible. Your interests may evolve, and that's perfectly fine.
- Avoid overcommitting to one interest at the outset. Exploration should be leisurely and enjoyable.
- Remember, mastery isn't the goal—joy is.

You'll know you've successfully identified and integrated your passions when you feel a renewed zest for life. Your days will have structure but also spontaneity, filled with activities that bring you happiness and satisfaction.

If you find yourself losing interest or feeling overwhelmed, step back. It's possible you've either not found the right passion or you're putting too much pressure on yourself. Revisit the exploration phase, and remember, this journey is personal and should be enjoyable.

Retirement is no longer just about winding down; it's about opening up new possibilities. It offers a unique opportunity to pursue passion and purpose in ways that were perhaps not possible earlier in life. By embracing this phase with an open mind and a spirit of adventure, retirees those who are about to retire can embark on a fulfilling journey of personal growth, contribution, and joy.

Let's learn how to turn your hobbies into opportunities in the next chapter.

10

Rule 7: Turn Hobbies into
Opportunities

****

*"My grandmother lived to 104 years old, and part of her success was she
woke up every morning to a brand new day. She said every morning is a
new gift. Her favorite hobby was collecting birthdays."*
- George Takei

The transition to retirement presents an unparalleled opportunity to redefine oneself. It's a time when your days ahead brim
with potential. Yet, amidst this newfound freedom, a significant challenge looms – the quest for purpose and meaning beyond the traditional confines of work and career.

The core of this challenge lies in the sudden expanse of unstruc-
tured time. Without the familiar rhythm of daily work commitments,
some find themselves adrift, grappling with a sense of loss or a dwin-
dling sense of purpose. Left unaddressed, this void can lead to feelings
of isolation, a decline in mental health, and a lack of fulfillment in
what are supposed to be the 'golden years.'

The transformation of hobbies and personal interests into avenues
for contribution, connection, and even income. The solution? To actively seek and create opportunities that not only align with one's

passions but also serve the larger community or even evolve into a lucrative endeavor.

The initial step towards this transformation involves a deep dive into one's hobbies and interests, followed by a strategic evaluation of how these can be leveraged. Whether it's the culinary arts, gardening, writing, or any other passion, the goal is to identify how these interests can be extended beyond personal enjoyment to create value for others.

For instance, a gardening enthusiast might consider starting a blog or YouTube channel to share their expertise, or even offer personalized garden design services. Alternatively, they could volunteer at community gardens or schools, imparting their knowledge to the next generation and fostering a love for the environment. The possibilities are as varied as the hobbies themselves.

Implementing this solution requires a structured approach. Begin by listing your hobbies and evaluating them based on three criteria: your level of expertise, your passion for the subject, and the potential for societal contribution or income generation. Next, research the avenues through which your hobby can be shared or monetized, and outline a plan to develop your skills further if necessary.

The efficacy of this approach is supported by numerous success stories. Take, for example, the retired teacher who turned her love for knitting into a small business, selling her creations online and at local craft fairs. Or the avid cyclist who started leading bike tours for tourists, combining his passion for cycling and his love for his city.

While transforming hobbies into opportunities is a promising solution, it's not without alternatives. Some may prefer to dive into entirely new fields, taking courses and acquiring new skills that can open up different paths for volunteer work or entrepreneurship. Others might opt for a more traditional part-time job in a field related to their interests, providing structure and additional income without the need for starting from scratch.

Have you considered the potential lying dormant in your hobbies? Picture the joy of sharing your passion with others, the fulfillment derived from contributing to your community, or the excitement of earning income from doing what you love. This isn't merely a dream but a tangible reality within your grasp.

In embracing this journey, remember that the aim is not just to fill your days but to enrich your life and the lives of those around you. As you walk on this path, let your hobbies light the way, transforming the golden years into a time of vibrant growth, contribution, and personal fulfillment.

You need to know a few aspects of life that makes you happy and joyous and it's important for you to build it in your retirement years. Let's discuss it in the next few chapters.

11

Leaving a Legacy

By embarking on the journey outlined in the preceding chapters, you have already taken significant strides towards redefining your golden years. Yet, the quest for a fulfilling retirement transcends the mere pursuit of hobbies and personal interests. It beckons towards a more profound horizon—the crafting of a lasting legacy that resonates beyond the confines of financial wealth. This chapter, "Leaving a Legacy," dares to promise you an exploration into the realms of mentorship, community service, and creative endeavors as avenues to imprint your mark on future generations.

Embark on this chapter with the assurance that by its conclusion, you will have gained insights into weaving a legacy rich with meaning, one that extends beyond the material to touch the lives of others in transformative ways. Through the power of mentorship, community service, and the magic of creative expression, In this chapter, we'll discover how to make your golden years an inspiration for future generations.

Mentorship emerges as a golden thread in this fabric, offering a unique blend of wisdom, experience, and guidance to the younger generation. Imagine the satisfaction derived from guiding a fledgling entrepreneur through the maze of business, bolstering a young writer's confidence, or sharing the intricacies of a cherished craft. These interactions not only enrich the lives of the mentees but also provide a profound sense of purpose and fulfillment to the mentor.

Community service stands as a proof to the strength of collective action. By lending your skills, time, and energy to local initiatives, you become a pillar of support in the edifice of your community. Whether it's revitalizing a public space, participating in educational programs, or supporting environmental conservation efforts, your contribution fosters a legacy of care, resilience, and unity.

Creative endeavors offer a canvas for expression that transcends time. Writing, painting, music, and other forms of art not only serve as a conduit for your inner voice but also leave a tangible legacy that can inspire, provoke thought, and bring beauty to the lives of others. Through your creations, you share a piece of your essence, etching your values, perspectives, and dreams into the collective memory of humanity.

Are you skeptical about the impact of these endeavors? Do doubts cloud your belief in the power of mentorship, community service, and creativity to forge a lasting legacy? Let these doubts dissolve as you consider the ripple effects of your actions. Each life you touch, directly or indirectly, carries forward a fragment of your legacy, multiplying its reach and impact across time and space.

Envision the transformation that awaits you. Picture a future where your contributions have shaped the lives of individuals, fortified the bonds within your community, and added to the cultural wealth of society. This is not a distant dream but a reality within your grasp, shaped by the choices and actions you take today.

In sealing your commitment to this journey, remember that the legacy you leave is not measured by material wealth but by the richness of your contributions to the world. Through mentorship, community service, and creative endeavors, you have the power to influence the future, leaving a legacy that echoes through generations.

I invite you to step boldly into this chapter of your life that offers unparalleled potential for impact. Let the pages that follow serve as your guide, illuminating the path towards a legacy that truly embodies the spirit of living a happy, healthy, and wealthy life.

12

New Paradigm: Redefining
Financial Success

"As I look back on my life, I realize that every time I thought I was being rejected from something good, I was actually being redirected to something better."
- Dr. Steve Maraboli

Money has a purpose. A stream of money should have your signature of purpose. In this chapter let's learn this aspect of money in more detail.

It's time to shift our perspective and embrace a more holistic approach to financial well-being– one that values not just the size of our bank accounts but the richness of our lives. This paradigm shift involves redefining success on our own terms, aligning our financial goals with our deepest values and aspirations. Under this new paradigm, we measure success not by the zeros in our net worth but by the impact we have on the world around us, the personal growth we experience, and the fulfillment we derive from our pursuits. It's about striking a balance between our financial aspirations and our overall well-being, ensuring that our quest for wealth does not come at the expense of our relationships, our health, or our sense of purpose.

Putting Values and Purpose First

Consider the example of Peace, a successful entrepreneur who built a thriving business from the ground up. Despite her impressive financial achievements, she found herself feeling unfulfilled and disconnected from her true passions. It wasn't until she took a step back and realigned her priorities with her core values that she truly found fulfillment. Peace decided to use her wealth and resources to support causes that were close to her heart, investing in sustainable initiatives and empowering underserved communities. By focusing on her purpose and the positive impact Peace discovered a sense of richness that extended far beyond her bank account.

Addressing Potential Objections

Some might argue that financial security is a fundamental human need, and that disregarding traditional wealth metrics is impractical or even irresponsible. However, this new paradigm does not negate the importance of financial planning or responsible money management. Instead, it encourages a more balanced approach, where financial goals are pursued in harmony with our overall well-being and our deeper sense of purpose. Others might question the feasibility of redefining success in a society that still heavily values material wealth and external markers of status. While this challenge is valid, it is precisely by challenging these societal norms that we can inspire lasting change. By leading by example and demonstrating the fulfillment that comes from a more holistic approach to financial well-being, we can inspire others to reevaluate their own definitions of success.

Embracing a Richer Life

To truly embrace this new paradigm of financial success, we must take proactive steps to align our financial choices with our values and aspirations. This might involve:

- Reevaluating our spending habits and prioritizing investments that align with our passions and contribute to our overall well-being.

- Pursuing career paths that not only provide financial stability but also allow us to make a positive impact and express our unique talents.

- Cultivating a mindset of gratitude and contentment, appreciating the abundance we already have in our lives, rather than constantly chasing more.

- Investing in experiences and relationships that enrich our lives and foster personal growth, rather than solely focusing on material possessions.

- Engaging in purposeful work, whether through volunteering, activism, or entrepreneurial endeavors that create positive change in the world around us.

By taking these steps, we can begin to redefine our relationship with money and embrace a richer, more fulfilling life – one that transcends the confines of arbitrary numbers and celebrates the true essence of prosperity.

In the end, the quest for financial success is not about amassing wealth for its own sake but about creating a life that is deeply fulfilling, purposeful, and aligned with our deepest values. By questioning the traditional metrics of wealth and embracing a more holistic approach, we can unlock a path to true prosperity – a richness of spirit, a depth of fulfillment, and a legacy that extends far beyond the digits in our bank accounts.

13

Learning to Unlearn

"Most successful people approach a book as though it has the potential to make them richer by information. They see every opportunity to train and educate themselves in new ways."
- Unknown

After retirement, you will expose to new information because of the extra time in your hand and this new information may clash with your pre-dominant beliefs. This chapter helps you on how to unlearn the old outdated pre-dominant beliefs or re-set your old setting. Let's learn more about it here.

You were raised with certain beliefs, exposed to specific information, and conditioned by the environments that shaped you. These early experiences cement the foundational layers of your knowledge base – a repository of ideas, assumptions, and perceptions that you carry forward into the world. While indispensable for navigating life's complexities, the very nature of these preconceived notions can become a hindrance, shackling you to outdated or inaccurate information.

Imagine your mind as a vast library, its shelves stacked with volumes of accumulated wisdom. Each book represents a concept, a belief, or a piece of knowledge ingrained within you. Over time, new editions emerge, revising and updating the original texts to reflect the latest insights and discoveries. Yet, the old editions, those tattered volumes you once devoured, remain stubbornly embedded in your psyche, their words etched into your neural pathways. This resistance to letting go of what you've known, this reluctance to discard the familiar in favor of the new, is a psychological barrier that impedes your ability to unlearn. Like a tenacious ivy, your preconceived notions cling to the walls of your understanding, obscuring the light of fresh perspectives and stifling the growth of your intellectual garden. The consequences of this resistance are far-reaching. Clinging to outdated information can lead to flawed decision-making, stunted personal growth, and a widening chasm between your understanding and the ever-evolving reality of the world around you. It is a

trap that ensnares even the most brilliant minds, rendering them captive to their own biases and limiting their capacity for intellectual renewal.

The Psychology of Unlearning

Unlearning is not merely a matter of erasing old information and replacing it with new; it is a complex psychological process that requires conscious effort and a willingness to confront the discomfort of cognitive dissonance. It demands that you challenge deeply ingrained beliefs, question long-held assumptions.

At the heart of this process lies the concept of cognitive dissonance – the mental discomfort experienced when new information contradicts your existing beliefs or values. This dissonance creates an internal conflict, a tug-of-war between the desire to cling to the familiar and the allure of embracing the unfamiliar. To unlearn, you must confront this dissonance head-on, acknowledging the tension between what you know and what you are being asked to accept. It is a journey fraught with emotional and psychological hurdles, as the very foundations upon which you have built your understanding are called into question.

Yet, within this discomfort lies the seed of growth, the potential for intellectual transformation. By mustering the courage to confront your cognitive dissonance, you create space for new insights to take root.

Strategies for Unlearning

Unlearning is not a passive process; it requires active engagement and a deliberate strategy. Here are some powerful techniques to help you embrace the art of unlearning:

1. Cultivate Intellectual Humility: Recognize that your knowledge is inherently limited and subject to revision. Approach new information with an open mind, shedding the arrogance of certainty and embracing the humility that allows you to question your own beliefs.

2. Seek Diverse Perspectives: Immerse yourself in a variety of viewpoints, challenging the echo chambers that reinforce your existing notions. Engage with individuals who hold differing beliefs, and actively seek out perspectives that contradict your own.

3. Practice Active Listening: When confronted with new information, resist the urge to immediately dismiss or defend. Instead, listen with an open heart and mind, allowing the new ideas to permeate your consciousness before formulating a response.

4. Embrace Discomfort: Recognize that unlearning is inherently uncomfortable, as it requires dismantling the familiar and embracing the unfamiliar. Lean into this discomfort, using it as a catalyst for growth and self-reflection.

5. Adopt a Growth Mindset: Cultivate a mindset that views learning as a continuous journey, rather than a destination. Embrace the idea that your understanding is ever evolving, and that unlearning is a necessary component of intellectual growth.

6. Practice Mindfulness: Cultivate a state of present-moment awareness, observing your thoughts and beliefs with a non-judgmental perspective. This mindful approach can help you recognize the

limitations of your own knowledge and the need for continuous re-newal.

By employing these strategies, you can create an environment con-ducive to unlearning, fostering the mental flexibility and resilience required to adapt to the ever-changing landscape of knowledge.

The Rewards of Unlearning

The process of unlearning may be arduous, but the rewards are profound. By shedding the shackles of outdated information and em-bracing the fluidity of knowledge, you unlock a world of intellectual richness and personal growth. Imagine a mind unencumbered by the weight of preconceived notions, a mind that dances with the rhythm of discovery, constantly reinventing itself in the face of new insights. This is the mind of the lifelong learner, the individual who embraces the art of unlearning as a catalyst for intellectual renewal.

With each layer of outdated knowledge shed, you create space for fresh perspectives to take root, allowing you to approach challenges with a renewed sense of clarity and insight. Your decision-making becomes more nuanced, your problem-solving more innovative, and your ability to adapt to change more resilient.

Moreover, the act of unlearning cultivates a profound sense of intellectual humility, a recognition that your understanding is ever-evolving and subject to revision. This humility fosters an openness to new ideas, a willingness to question your own assumptions, and a deep respect for the complexity of knowledge itself.

In essence, unlearning is not a passive process of forgetting; it is an active embrace of intellectual growth, a conscious decision to shed the limiting shackles of preconceived notions in favor of the boundless potential of new understanding. It is a journey that demands courage, resilience, and a deep commitment to the pursuit of truth – a journey that ultimately enriches not only your intellect but your very essence as a human being.

14

Charting Uncharted Waters

****

"Do not go where the path may lead; go instead where there is no path and leave a trail."

- Ralph Waldo Emerson

The retirement years are full of new life. We human are not train to accept the changes or train to chart on uncharted waters. Let's learn how to overcome on this problem in this chapter.

The Myth of the Linear Path

Is success truly found on a straight, unwavering path, or does it lie in the detours and unexpected turns that define our journeys?

The notion of a linear career trajectory has long been ingrained in our collective consciousness. From a young age, we're taught to set goals, climb the proverbial ladder, and strive for a linear ascent towards success. However, this narrow perspective fails to capture the dynamic, ever-evolving nature of personal and professional growth. In reality, the path to fulfillment is often winding, unpredictable, and rife with pivots and course corrections.

The problem with clinging to a rigid, linear mindset is that it constrains our ability to adapt and thrive in an era of unprecedented change. In a world where industries rise and fall, where disruptive technologies reshape entire sectors, and where the skills in demand are in constant flux, a one-track approach to career development can leave us ill-equipped to navigate the complexities of the modern workforce.

*"The future belongs to those who learn more skills and combine them in creative ways." - **Robert Green***

Many people fall into the trap of pursuing a singular vision of success, sacrificing flexibility and exploration in favor of a narrow, predefined trajectory. They cling to the idea that success is a straight line, ignoring the myriad opportunities for growth and reinvention that lie off the beaten path. This myopic approach can lead to stagnation, unfulfillment, and a failure to capitalize on emerging possibilities.

Instead, we should embrace a non-linear approach to career development – one that celebrates curiosity, adaptability, and a willingness to pivot in pursuit of growth and fulfillment. This alternative perspective recognizes that true success is not a destination but a journey of continuous learning, evolving interests, and the courage to explore uncharted territories.

Critics may argue that a non-linear approach to career development is inherently risky, lacking the stability and structure of a traditional, linear trajectory. They might contend that frequent pivots and changes in direction could lead to a lack of focus or depth in any particular area, potentially hindering long-term success.

However, this criticism fails to acknowledge the rapidly evolving nature of the modern workforce and the value of adaptability in navigating its complexities. Rather than being a liability, a non-linear approach equips individuals with the agility and versatility to thrive in an ever-changing landscape. By cultivating a growth mindset and embracing continuous learning, professionals can develop the resilience and transferable skills necessary to succeed in a variety of roles and industries.

To embrace a non-linear path to success, consider the following actionable steps:

1. Cultivate a growth mindset: Approach your career with curiosity and a willingness to continuously learn and evolve. Embrace challenges as opportunities for growth, and seek out experiences that push you beyond your comfort zone.
2. Develop transferable skills: Focus on building a diverse skillset that transcends any single role or industry. Invest in developing critical thinking, problem-solving, communication, and adaptability – skills that are valuable across a wide range of contexts.
3. Build a network of diverse perspectives: Surround yourself with individuals from varied backgrounds and industries. This exposure to different perspectives and experiences can open your eyes to new possibilities and inspire pivots you may not have considered otherwise.
4. Remain open to unexpected opportunities: Rather than adhering to a rigid plan, maintain an open mindset and be willing to explore unexpected opportunities that align with your evolving interests and aspirations.
5. Embrace lifelong learning: Commit to continuous education and skill development, whether through formal channels or self-directed learning. This will ensure that you remain relevant and adaptable in the face of rapid change.
6. Reframe setbacks as stepping stones: When faced with challenges or detours, view them as opportunities for growth and learning, rather than failures or dead ends. These experiences can shape your resilience and inform future pivots.

In conclusion, the path to true success is rarely linear. By embracing a non-linear approach to life development, we can unlock a world of possibilities, cultivate adaptability, and forge a journey of continuous growth and fulfillment. Success is not a destination but a journey of exploration, reinvention, and the courage to embrace the unexpected turns that define our unique paths.

15

Be a Mentor

****

"A mentor is someone who sees more talent and ability within you, than you see in yourself, and helps bring it out of you."
- Bob Proctor

We discussed about mentoring in the chapter 'Opportunities Awaiting in Retirement' at a small scale. Let's dive into it in more detail here.

How to adopt the path of mentorship?

A mentor can create a huge talent pool for the country and that can be translated into a human asset. You can choose the path of mentorship and serve your country after retirement. Let's discuss about various aspects of mentorship in this chapter.

1. The Importance of Mentorship: An Evidence-Based Anchoring

In the ever-changing tides of professional waters, mentors serve as beacons of guidance, illuminating paths forward and anchoring us amidst the currents of uncertainty. Their wisdom, forged through the crucible of experience, provides a steadying force – a lighthouse amidst the fog of career navigation. This chapter delves into the profound impact of mentorship, anchoring its analysis in the robust evidence that underscores the invaluable role these relationships play in fostering professional growth, resilience, and fulfillment.

2. The Claim: Mentors as Career Anchors

Mentorship is a potent force, capable of transforming careers and unlocking untapped potential. These relationships offer a lifeline to those navigating uncharted waters, providing invaluable guidance, support, and insights that can steer professionals toward greater success and personal growth. By cultivating mentoring connections, individuals gain access to a wealth of knowledge, experience, and perspectives that can anchor their journey and help them navigate even the most turbulent career seas.

3. The Evidence: A Wealth of Research

Numerous studies have illuminated the tangible benefits of mentorship, solidifying its position as a cornerstone of professional development and career advancement. A comprehensive analysis by Sun Microsystems found that mentees were 20% more likely to receive promotions than their non-mentored counterparts, underscoring the impact of these relationships on upward mobility. Furthermore, a Gallup study revealed that employees who had received mentoring were significantly more engaged and productive, contributing to both personal and organizational success.

4. Delving Deeper: The Mentorship Effect

The power of mentorship extends far beyond mere career advancement or monetary gains. These relationships foster a rich tapestry of benefits that ripple across personal and professional domains. Mentors serve as sounding boards, offering objective perspectives and guidance that can help mentees navigate complex challenges and make informed decisions. Their counsel can be invaluable in navigating ethical quandaries.

Moreover, mentors can impart invaluable lessons in leadership, communication, and emotional intelligence – skills that are increasingly prized in the modern workforce. By modeling these traits and providing constructive feedback, mentors help mentees develop the soft skills that can propel them toward positions of influence and impact.

5. Considering Counterpoints: The Pitfalls of Mentorship

While the benefits of mentorship are well-documented, it would be remiss not to acknowledge potential pitfalls or challenges. Power dynamics within mentoring relationships can sometimes lead to unhealthy dependencies or imbalances, hindering personal growth or fostering toxic environments. Additionally, mismatched expectations or incompatible personalities can undermine the effectiveness of these connections, rendering them unproductive or even detrimental.

6. Addressing Counterpoints: Fostering Healthy Mentorship

These potential pitfalls, however, can be mitigated through intentional efforts to establish healthy boundaries, clear expectations, and open communication. By fostering an environment of mutual respect, trust, and accountability, mentors and mentees can cultivate relationships that empower personal growth while maintaining appropriate boundaries.

Furthermore, organizations can implement robust mentorship programs that prioritize thoughtful matching processes, ongoing support, and training to ensure these connections thrive on a foundation of ethical conduct and mutual benefit.

7. Further Evidence: The Ripple Effect

The impact of mentorship extends far beyond the individuals directly involved, reverberating through organizations and industries. A study by Deloitte found that companies with robust mentoring programs experienced higher retention rates, increased employee engagement, and improved knowledge transfer – all factors that contribute to organizational success and competitiveness.

Moreover, mentors themselves often report profound personal growth and fulfillment through these relationships, experiencing a renewed sense of purpose and an opportunity to pay it forward by shaping the next generation of leaders.

8. Real-World Applications: Anchoring Careers in Mentorship

The transformative power of mentorship is exemplified in countless real-world success stories. Consider the journey of Emily, a budding entrepreneur who found herself adrift in the turbulent waters of starting her own business. Through a serendipitous connection, she forged a mentoring relationship with a seasoned industry veteran, who not only provided invaluable guidance on navigating the complexities of entrepreneurship but also introduced her to a network of potential investors and collaborators.

Or take the case of Jacob, a mid-career professional grappling with stagnation and disillusionment. His mentor, a former colleague, helped him rediscover his passion, explore lateral career moves, and develop the confidence to chart a new course – one that reignited his sense of purpose and fulfillment.

These stories illustrate how mentors can anchor careers, providing the support, insights, and connections that empower individuals to navigate even the most tumultuous professional tides.

Conclusion: Casting Anchors of Mentorship:

In the vast expanse of the career ocean, mentors serve as crucial anchors, providing stability, guidance, and support. By embracing the power of these relationships, we tap into a wellspring of wisdom and experience that can steer us through the currents of uncertainty and propel us toward greater heights of personal and professional growth.

So, let us cast our anchors of mentorship, forging connections that will not only enrich our careers but also shape the lives of those who will one day follow in our wake. In the end, it is through these relationships that we create a legacy – a living tapestry of knowledge, wisdom, and guidance that will anchor generations to come and one can achieve this feat only after retirement.

16

How to Transform
Obstacles into
Opportunities

****

*"Every adversity, every failure, every heartache carries with it the seed
of an equal or greater benefit."*
- Napoleon Hill

L ife is full of adversities and you need to deal with it. We'll face it
even after retirement. Let's learn how to tackle this life situation
in this chapter.

What if adversity were the key to unlocking our greatest potential? You've encountered obstacles that seemed insurmountable, challenges that threatened to bury your dreams beneath an avalanche of setbacks and failures. In those moments of despair, it might have felt like the world was conspiring against you, ruthlessly demolishing the foundations you had so meticulously constructed. Yet, what if these very obstacles, these seemingly insurmountable barriers, were not impediments but catalysts for personal growth and transformation?

The way we perceive and respond to adversity holds the power to shape our destiny. Too often, we view challenges as adversaries to be vanquished, obstacles to be overcome through sheer force of will. Yet, this perspective overlooks the profound lessons and opportunities for growth that lie within the crucible of hardship. By reframing our understanding of adversity, we can unlock a wellspring of resilience and self-discovery, transforming our greatest trials into the fertile soil from which our most extraordinary achievements will blossom.

Paralysis in the Face of Adversity: When faced with overwhelming challenges, it's all too easy to succumb to paralysis, allowing fear and self-doubt to take root within our psyche. We fixate on the magnitude of the obstacle, magnifying its perceived impossibility until it looms larger than life, casting a shadow of despair over our dreams and aspirations. In this state of paralysis, we become trapped in a cycle of inaction, our momentum stifled by the weight of our own limiting beliefs.

Common Misconceptions and Ineffective Approaches: It is common for people to try to overcome adversity by gritting their teeth and pushing forward with unwavering determination. While admirable, this approach often overlooks the deeper lessons and opportunities for growth embedded within the challenge itself. Others may adopt a defeatist mindset, resigning themselves to their perceived fate and surrendering to it. Both of these extremes fail to harness the transformative power of adversity, neglecting the profound personal evolution that can arise from navigating and embracing life's avalanches.

Embracing the Avalanche: We must embrace a paradigm shift – a fundamental reframing of our relationship with hardship. Rather than viewing challenges as obstacles to be overcome or adversaries to be defeated, we must learn to perceive them as catalysts for growth, opportunities to forge resilience and self-mastery. When we approach adversity with this mindset, the very avalanches that once threatened to bury us become the building blocks of our strength.

Real-Life Triumphs: Turning avalanches into foundations this perspective is not mere rhetoric; it is a truth embodied by countless individuals who have transformed their greatest trials into their most extraordinary triumphs. Consider the story of Oprah Winfrey, who rose from a childhood marred by abuse and poverty to become one of the most influential voices of our time, using her platform to empower millions. Or the tale of J.K. Rowling, who wrote the first Harry Potter book while navigating the depths of poverty and depression, only to have her creation become a global phenomenon that ignited the imaginations of countless readers.

These narratives of resilience and triumph are not isolated instances but rather testament to the innate human capacity to transmute adversity into fuel for personal transformation. They serve as living proof that the very avalanches that threaten to bury us can, in fact, become the foundations upon which we construct our most extraordinary lives.

Addressing Objections: Overcoming self-doubt and fear yet, even as we acknowledge the potential for growth within adversity, doubts and fears may linger. "How can I possibly overcome this challenge when it feels so insurmountable?" "What if I'm not strong enough to weather the storm?" These whispers of self-doubt are natural, but they must be confronted and silenced by the unwavering determination to grow from our trials.

The truth is that resilience is not an innate trait but a muscle that must be exercised and strengthened through repeated exposure to adversity. Each obstacle we face, each avalanche we confront, provides an opportunity to fortify our resolve and deepen our faith in our ability to overcome. By facing our fears head-on and embracing the discomfort of growth, we cultivate a resilience that becomes an unshakable foundation for our future triumphs.

The Path Forward: Embracing your avalanches to embark on this journey of personal transformation, you must first make a conscious choice to shift your perspective. Instead of viewing challenges as obstacles to be overcome, reframe them as opportunities for growth, as catalysts for the expansion of your resilience and self-mastery.

Embrace the discomfort that accompanies adversity, for it is within this discomfort that the seeds of personal evolution are planted. Seek out the lessons embedded within each challenge, the insights that will fortify your character and deepen your understanding of yourself and the world around you.

Surround yourself with a supportive network of individuals who can provide encouragement and guidance as you navigate life's avalanches. These allies can offer a fresh perspective, reminding you of your strength when self-doubt clouds your vision, and celebrating your progress as you emerge from each challenge more resilient and self-assured.

Above all, cultivate a mindset of gratitude for the adversities that cross your path. For it is within these crucibles of hardship that your true mettle is forged, your character honed, and your potential unlocked. Embrace life's avalanches not as obstacles to be overcome but as the raw materials from which you will construct the foundations of your most extraordinary life.

17

Conclusion

"Nothing will work unless you do."
- Maya Angelou

Here, the reader is asked to stop and reflect on a content of this book, that even though finished on paper, but has all idea to give a push for your retirement. Ultimately, the end of the book is just the start of a deeper insight that the content we share reflect our deepest selves and the infinite ways we can experience the life of retirement. We begin with the chapter on why to retire then discussed all the seven golden rules of retirement one after the other. Then we move to the part that explains the various other factor related to retirement. This book is like a tool that helps you to peep into your retirement years if you are yet to retire.

The book covers not only the financial aspect of retirement but also the mental aspect in following ways:

1. How to unlearn and learn new things?
2. How to chart on uncharted waters?
3. How to earn money that has a purpose?
4. How to choose the path of mentorship after retirement?
5. How to turn obstacles into opportunities?

Our lifetime is just a flash on the timeline of universe. You need to bring the urgency in your life work and that can be accomplished only after the retirement.

One can generate ideas if he or she is free from any entitlement to work, and the world needs more people who generate ideas. We are not born to pay the bills but to live a life of full potential that not only helps people live a great life but also helps our planet to be a better place. You can make it possible if you choose the path of retirement.

Feel free to give me feedback on this book on my email ID emmanzvada@gmail.com.

www.ingramcontent.com/pod-product-compliance
Lightning Source LLC
Chambersburg PA
CBHW071514210326
41597CB00018B/2754